THE CLOSE WORLD

The Close World

Poems

Adin Thayer

TEBOT BACH • HUNTINGTON BEACH • CALIFORNIA • 2021

Front cove: Nightlight photo: Nathan Carpenter
Back cover: Lake Kivu at border between Rwanda and Democratic Republic
of the Congo. Credit: Adin Thayer
Author's photo: Jeff McQueen
Book design by: Russel Davis, Gray Dog Press, Spokane, WA

ISBN-10: 1-939678-87-0
ISBN-13: 978-1-939678-87-4

A Tebot Bach book
Tebot Bach, Welsh for little teapot, is a Nonprofit Public Benefit
Corporation, which sponsors workshops, forums, lectures, and
publications. Tebot Bach books are distributed by Small Press
Distribution.

The Tebot Bach Mission: Advancing literacy, strengthening
community, and transforming life experiences with the power of
poetry through readings, workshops, and publications.

This book is made possible by a generous donation from
Steven R. and Lera B. Smith.

www.tebotbach.org

Contents

PART II

In the deserts of the heart / let the healing fountains start

PART III

These are the sparks

Part I

. . . let me love what I cannot know . . .
—W. S. Merwin, "To The Rain"

A Question as the Sun Comes Up

Indeterminant morning
mottled and cool, leaves tentative
on the sycamore. There's traffic far away
and vague, north and south
on 91, trucks hauling fruit, Budweiser,
cargo for Walmart;

and buses,   a few travelers
with windows for pillows
will be missing sunrise
which is making a brief coral
and gold announcement.
But drivers going east toward Boston
will see it and maybe one will sigh
and feel inexplicably hopeful,
one may murmur
into the morning air,
and some will be lost
in thought, as we say,

as you could say
I am, wondering
whether the way the sun
has of rising heeded or not
with such heart-wrenching
extravagance has ever stopped
a blow from landing,
or stayed a trigger finger.

Honey from Rwanda

Tangled scarlet canopies draped high
above shade, vines in ditches, upright oleander,

bougainvillea dimmed by dust;
in coffee fields on the sulfurous flanks of volcanoes,

down in the rice valleys,   blood gone
from the ground still the tomb of bone,

a child's jacket upended with a hoe. Years
later the earth is still mineral red,

pierced by the push of maize, bananas,
sorghum and beans grown to feed

children, bus drivers, men in crowded cells
and above it all, the brilliant blossoms

still hungry to be plundered,
command the bees: take, produce. Feed.

A Question and an Answer

I asked how it could be that you sang
as though these hard chairs
were still trees overhead
and you a bird
among berries, while
your children lie in rows
underground in wood boxes
slapped together by the thousands,
beside rows of manioc
and maize, as though all those
children were still singing too,

and you said one thing to me: *We pray.*

At Times My Heart

at times my heart
    is all ashes,
            the quiet residue
    of flaming starts,
the burned bones
    of never quite and then
            it was too late, the humble
    powdery remains
of love so alive

    it bursts like birds   startled
            from their branches

            giving voice
                to the air itself.

Neighbors

In 1994 when every choice
was forced, he killed her children.
She had run with the youngest
as he entered the yard, and crouched
under sorghum.

This morning a coral-breasted
bird sits in the eucalyptus,
her liquid solo lifting
darkness from the garden.

The rains should come
soon, pounding banana trees and tin roofs.
Today he hoes rows for beans
and corn. She wrings out
the blue uniform her daughter wears
to school, and hangs it
over the hedge.

The field he's planting
belongs to her. At church she hears
words: atonement, forgiveness,   a pair
of gestures some accomplish.
She sings.

The rows stretch back
behind her house, corn and beans
hoed in where the sorghum was.
He sits in the dim late afternoon waiting
for rain, his old feet cracked,
and drinks banana beer.

Encounter with a Mother in Rwanda

she held tight as though to a diminishing other half
and rocked   bent

among passers-by   rocked
like a tree in wailing wind   she said

nothing
except with her bony body   which said

I will never see him again
            and I held her in return   as though

for him   in the new country of checkbook
            and snow

she said no words
as I gave her the shoes he had packed

in a box   her face a folded stone
that once had bent to him

who still knew the size of her foot
and whom she wouldn't see

again   except in the pictures I had snapped
before leaving

The Night the Mosquito Net Is Breached

There's a thin invisible drone
from left in the dark
and right in the dark   airy

segmented messengers
touch down light as kisses
for a baby asleep   and *bite*

I swat and swat all night
deprived of dreams, only
a nasal hum for company in this world,

only a message of hunger
unsated   but then insomnia ascends
into the reaches of stillness everywhere,

people on pallets and mattresses
in the town around me
lifted from their separate lives

together into a cloud of shared quiet
that hovers above us
like a weightless quilt I wouldn't have felt

without the messengers
pocking my face
and arms with their delicate venom

But for her Clear Voice

Her arm ends
somewhere below the elbow.
The rest fell into the swamp downhill from their village
one night   which would be unspeakable
but for her clear voice.
It had been too dark to see faces.

The man in the chair to her left this quiet afternoon
didn't sever her arm.
Eyes down he listens while she explains he was the one
who slashed her shoulder while the baby
lay nearby.

After prison and years of gaping dreams
he had said to her on the street
I did this,
pointing to her shoulder.   She had fallen
to the ground again, and this time
he fell too.

Now their quiet voices fill a mud room,
using up the air.
Her husband has listened from a corner.   Standing,
his arm lifted he prays
a long prayer   before silence rises around us.

The Sharp Embrace

One loss / folds itself inside another
—Jane Hirshfield, **Come Thief**

The way thunder
detonates in the pulse
of the soldier
back home.

Or the opening notes
of a Mozart concerto
catch you by surprise
as you pass an open window
and the evenings
of childhood ascend,
how you listened from bed,
both alone and a part
of some harmony.

The force of love revealed
through the severance
loss enforces. The soldier
who will never
not have killed,
the widow left
with a jacket she can't let go,
the walker transposed by music,
all harbor the grain
of new love, abraded by the sharp
embrace of the relinquished.

Potatoes, Wood in Eastern Congo

Sun rises from Lake Kivu, fishermen glide,
pulling their nets.

A woman pulls wood on her back bent
like a fist. She is one of many,

femmes transporteuses, they're called.
Foot by foot she leans forward

in a passing crowd downhill from the café
where a waiter whisks

away my plate and offers me Nescafé,
smoothly impersonal.

How many solitudes by the sparkling lake?
And what are the words

for a woman harnessed to wood?
She stumbles in mud,

the wood falls
from its cloth cradle as the crowd trudges

around her. Potatoes,
shoes, today it's wood, the patterned cloth

keeps it anchored around her forehead.
A few francs.

Lake Kivu

The late sun is veiled
and through its fine mesh
the lake gathers depth.

Light splinters
on the water, and sinks
in mountain crevasses.

I sit at a metal table
beside the lake laid like a drawn breath
between the fields

of Rwanda and the dense forest
of Congo, a boundary
where terror prowls,

its footfall soft from behind.
Everywhere we are given beauty,
and oh,   *though it could wake us,*

         it sinks with the sun.

Boys in the Street in Bujumbura, Burundi

Heads down, eight or ten of them
moved in unison as though each was a piece
of some living whole. The shreds
flapping against their legs
were the color of dirt.
Around them lay the town
beige with dust, color of milky coffee,
still as a movie set through which a troupe
of extras loped from one scene to the next.

I sat invisible above them on a balcony
just big enough to hold a metal chair,
at my feet a thermos
I was draining cup by cup. Any minute
the sun would rise. The owner
of the kiosk for batteries and headphones
would open the iron-barred door
and put a basket of plastic sandals
out front.

~ ~ ~ ~ ~

The boys thin as pencils
had slept somewhere
on the street, and now moved
somewhere else at a hungry pace.
Later I would eat food put before me
at a meeting and then fly home.

~ ~ ~ ~ ~

Years later the boys appear
in memory, still passing
in silence, still just before sunrise.
How tired they must have been.
I look carefully.
The smallest has fallen
behind, and another one, maybe
his brother, drops back
to take his hand.
They pass by, not one left behind.

Sunset Day by Day

With a smile a young woman places a glass
of beer on the red plastic table I choose

whenever it's free, the one near the edge
of the lake.   The smallest habit can anchor a person

far from home. Elbows on *this* table,
soap placed just so back in the shaded room,

the book within reach in the dark.
Goats nibble and bleat under bushes,

while high above eucalyptus wave quietly
left and right.   Sleep comes early

in the profound rural quiet that falls
not long after dark in places with few lights,

so far from home life becomes simple –
        soap   book   sunset

Numbers

I slept 6 hours, waking once
in darkness.

I saw 2 gulls sailing through clouds,
and heard 7 peals from a church

in town make morning audible.
I saw 13 magazine covers

in the checkout line
at Stop & Shop yesterday,

and heard a siren blast at least 8 times
as I walked to the car.

I see 6 trees through a window
and 3 leaves straining

in wind on the knuckle of an oak limb.
I can't see

3,000,000 people beginning to starve
in Africa, although I heard

the number clearly on the radio.
I can't hear a single 1

of their voices.
I just know they're there.

Some Writers in Burundi Compose a Radio Drama in Which the Past Is Present

sun enters the garden surrounded
by birdsong   branches
tremble   the subject
is mass slaughter and those
whose parents survived or did not are dressing

in their rooms   preparing to write a story
about mass slaughter and those who survive
and what they make of the history held
in their bodies   they laugh
at the knots the story makes   as though to break
a spell   but silence enters the room
as they decide what to do with bodies   silence

containing grandparents who might have been slashed
by or slashed their neighbors
                each day they dress
with care   coiffed   and slow of gait   they laugh
as though laughter was food   and shrug
we go on

    in the drama they are writing from life:
        the youth demand answers
            from their parents; though they fear the caves
            in their aging eyes they must know;
        a body is found with a note: *back off!*
        a girl tells how her father, who she will learn
            is not her father, hides from his deeds in the woods;
        another reveals the day as a child
            soldier he led rebels to a family to be killed; later
            he will know whose family it was and face her

and on the story goes
and the laughter at lunch   is this too much I wonder
and they look at me: *little you know* they imply
as on we go

The Close World

The sun arrives
and birds re-establish
their frontiers,
the cat ends her wild travels
and winds into a bud
of sleep. The newspaper
lies there, its columns of lines.

I unfold it
to read what happened
while I slept. Details
of an explosion: numbers
tally bodies
in a marketplace.

~ ~ ~

By now it's afternoon there,
workers must be cleaning up,
resetting the stalls,
gathering produce
where it fell.   Here
the cat will sleep all morning.

Spring in Sarajevo

The hills rise as dawn becomes day.
Houses crowd along roads
that wind up to the hilltops
where snipers had shivered
in snow, practicing their aim on citizens
hurrying for bread.

Three winters: down below
a boy and girl
dart from a doorway.
One falls, one runs.

Today years later spring shows
on the faces of coffee drinkers,
their café chairs scattered in the town square.
People huddle and smoke in chill sun,
coffee comes with a Turkish candy,
a jelly square dusted with powdery sugar,
beside it on the dish.

The hills crown the city.
On one, gardens poke up outside
kitchen windows, on the next, a flock
of crosses, acres of white crosses,
some already tilting
the way grave markers do over time
though it hasn't been long.
The markers say 1993,
1994, 1993, 1995,
as though they fell in unison.
Neighborhoods of citizens
who bled out on the cobbles

of successive civilizations lie now
in neighborhoods of crosses
white like the late snow banked
along the roads winding up to the hills
where the sun rises
and the opposite hills
where it sets.

Say No Bird

almost silence   one bird at the edge
of a field with one note
repeated it seems at random   because
you are listening you notice what could seem
an absence
of pattern
but isn't

or say no bird   only
the stillness of table plank
and water glass   last year's fly
on the sill   say the hush
is alive
an unframed window   not that only the loved
live there   but that in it nothing
is absent   the unloved   the despised
also dwell

suppose we live within
its all-presence together   breathing together
in the silence
of the afterlives of all our years

Part II

Redbuds by the Road Today

Like fireworks   if fireworks blushed as they burst
five   six   seven explosions in a row

if explosions were quiet   the way these echo
softly through the woods   if an echo

was something felt in the bones of the face
before it smiles   the way smiling feels

when the past arrives with grace   they're only trees
elevating what the magenta buds

need to light up the shadows
cast by woods   and the shadow cast by a moment

when a mother now dead for years
was alive   and drove with her daughter

down a rural road past redbuds
and sighed with joy although they didn't pause

Something with Echoes

I wanted to give you
something I would miss.

My mother's measuring cup –
bent tin –
with it would go her coarse bread
and its braided crust.

Her sweater –
the one I'm wearing –
you see what I mean?

It's only a thing
you grab when you need it
but it clings like love.
Forgive me, for wanting you
to have it.

Garden My Body Suddenly Remembers

redwing screes from a reed
wake something not memory,

not nostalgia, some transposition
to a patch of dirt, two rows

of popcorn, two of desire,
desire to produce, and today,

to be there again
and choose again

maybe something that would grow –
small packet of possibility

kneeling in dirt by the house
already pagan to the core

The Sleeping Porch

Layered into my interior archeology
was a constituent sense of being combined

within a world   belonging
like yeast in bread

wrapped in a thin sheet
on a sagging sleeping porch skirting the front

of a mountain house in North Carolina.
Window screens scooped by age

but intact   and a row of beds   all of us
asleep on concave mattresses that sank into valleys

in the middle. As I lay on the end awake
with the silver glazed

cake of moon   the sleepers around me
breathing into the dark   solitude knew it had me

for life and was settling into my young body   confident
it too had something to offer.

Gathering Place

Either it was lonely childhood or something more interesting. Animals died all around us, killed mostly by fathers driving too fast to drinks at the end of their days after the war. They hit squirrels and dogs, sometimes a toad squashed thin as a picture with real glistening guts. Cats killed birds, a baby snake.

Each I scooped into my hands and took to the animal graveyard in the woods behind my house. To anyone passing it was a scatter of stones under a pine, one for the mangled chipmunk, one for the bird smashed on a windshield, flesh and minute bones.

Childhood enacting what it wanted to believe – that world where every life had value. That folly that didn't want to die.

A Child in Virginia in the '50s

Everyone I saw was white
except Betty Weaver
who ironed on Thursdays,
and the boy who stacked boxes
behind the produce
at Kroger's market
who was as dark
as our dining room table.
My third-grade book
of History taught Appomattox
without the story of skin.

Everyone I spoke to was white
but Betty, who was quiet
as she pressed my father's shirts.
Once I went with my mother
to take her home,
down a dirt road
to a gray wood cabin
as big as our living room.
I couldn't see an ironing board.
In her dim home
something changed
the eyes I saw with. Then
there was a before and an after.

Time's Secret

why   as we move
toward the end of things

do their beginnings
     rise like stars

light reaching
     from a time

when what is past
     was still a threshold?

Dixie

a past in which cotton was a globed and gleaming
king in a field combed by shoulders bright with sweat

soil the most beautiful of red   our soil
our folded mountains strewn with trillium
and trembling redbud   our attunement to its beauty
and the sharp smell
of decay   red seeping into children
who smell the story we have striven
not to tell

Sling the Statue

> Lynchburg, Virginia 1957

It was a favorite game:
if you were *it*

you took each player one at a time
by the wrist. You swung as hard as you could

in a circle and let them go
stumbling to a dead stop

they had to hold as the next was swung
and the next   arms out   back bent

freeze!
And the first to move

was the loser.   We were caught in the pose
of someone else's force.

We had no horse, no musket, no stone-grey
eyes gazing over the fields

of defeat.
We played unseeing

near the unseeing eyes of statues
it seemed would stand forever,

never the first to move,
never the losers.

The Fence Inside

> Integration of the schools but not the pools,
> Lynchburg, Virginia 1961

The pool was our summer –
cannonballs
towels on hot concrete
and the Beach Boys over the intercom –
we basted in the languorous days'
    secretions.

    As we lounged
in our chlorinated universe straps down
tanning evenly everywhere
with Coppertone, city leaders
made decisions. In the fierce heat of July
    school looming
    they locked the gate.

    In the part of town we never saw
another gate shut   and all those kids
    stood stunned like us,

    all of us barred
from the water we craved. Suddenly
two tall   chain-link   padlocked
            fences
    forbade we touch.
    The grown-ups got quiet.

    In September they put us side by side
in homeroom. His name was William.
The fences   the ones we saw
and the ones we didn't   had worked.
    My body was scared of his.

Jim Crow

You didn't notice it,
the way some people stood
aside as you passed, the way
bodies didn't touch.

There was never one touch
unless you had a maid or a cook.
Skin passed skin in the street
and tightened like the faces

of grownups. Eyes stole a look
or tried not to, or maybe
you just looked outright
at whoever you wanted to,

since you owned the world.
You didn't know where the jail was.
It wasn't like they weren't there.
It was like they weren't there.

It was like they were so there
that a knot tied inside – you didn't notice
you were knotted together
by not touching.

Appomattox

Still a modest settlement in the seedy fields
of central Virginia somnolent on the April afternoon
we arrive, five sisters with our mother,
thirty miles from our childhood home.

Here's where the grade school buses parked
while we the young were transfused
with the story of blood.
We are quiet in a ghost town shrill
with murmurs.

There's a talk for visitors.
Back out in the pouring sun we separate,
a sigh for valor from one,
from another the pursed lips of shame,
refusing that torn banner another way
of being Southern. The mother who never left.
Fractures craze our surface from within.

We fall into a vacuum of words, trailing
along the split-rail sided path the visitors follow
past the iron-potted kitchens,
the neighborly houses, church, slave cabins,
the room for ceremonial occasions,

each remembering the society of our childhood,
each with her own bitter taste.

Tree Fall, Bark Rot

Secretive field,
ruby shoulder of daybreak,

desire aches to hold,
to be wanted.

But the world belongs to itself,
does not give back.

It may be held only as stone,
as water. It is given to be loved

and give nothing
in reply but the redwing

in swinging grass, moss
glow under cracked leaves.

This is enough, tree-fall,
bark rot, anemone

like a moth hovering
above spring's debris.

Writing About Virginia

Try, she said,
to write about how the fields reach
        toward the mountains
like children wanting to be picked up,
stretching for shoulders
        they'll never ride
                or leave.

Try, she said,
to write about the hills
        that could hoist your spirits
                over any grief
        or into it.

Once,   try
to leave out the bodies
        moving in rows of tobacco   or bent
layering rose colored brick
        story by story and hauling wood from the forest
                for columned porches,
say how
        that earth would always be the only dirt
                you'd care to know about.
Stained plum,
        streaked ochre. Corn fields,
                mountains raised around us
        by something mighty.

But the red earth bore a marriage
    of richer and poorer indissoluble
        as night and star.
The ink of a story
    where some stand with bourbon
        on their spacious porches
while others absorb from the mineral earth
    singing, signals that rise over boxwoods
        and brick walkways up through French windows
            and right through the rooms and out back,
through the smoke house,
    the icehouse,
        and over the cabins and then the fields
            to the mountains and away.

Something I Didn't Know but Also Did

We were trudging up Greybeard Mountain,
heat pouring
off a North Carolina rhododendron canopy around us,
a train of cousins.
The stream where we hopped rocks roiled below
to the right of our path,
and someone saw a water moccasin sliding
like liquid through the leaves at the water's edge.
I was five, leaning to see.

Then I was in the air
suspended in my father's arms, dangling
in space above the snake,   wild
as a rabbit hung
on a hawk's talon.

Put me down! I cried
and kicked,
eyes shut.   Then my body knew something
I wouldn't know for years.

How else could he,
who sang us to sleep and cooked our scrambled eggs,
hold my thin breathless body over a precipice
above a gliding serpent, if not
to prepare me for what he had seen and,
surviving, half forgotten?

Vigil

Nina called our father up from the table in the garden
to where the six-foot oily coil of copperhead
stared at her.

Then, head severed, the snake lay
on the patio out back. We put on our nightgowns.

It stretched on stone   the long body writhing
headless
below the white and pink-red flowers
on apple branches outside our upstairs window,
        still moving as it was buried

in drifting blossoms.   Blood and garden
and the porch light on the long finally still length
of shimmering animal.

Pitch It Out

Our mother used the fine things
that came her way.
If it breaks, it breaks, she said.
Pitch it out, she'd say,
if she couldn't glue it.

Painstakingly she wrote
in the middle of the night,
year after year, poem by poem
unscrolling the past.

It's funny how a child hears
an instruction.
Pitch it out, she said,
as though she meant, *never let me go*.

Freesias From My Father

They came in a box
with a card handwritten years after his stroke,
lines of wobbling words
specifically to me.

They lay under paper as thin as thought
that extended my suspense an extra
second while fragrance
lifted through the mud room where I stood
on the morning of a nondescript
February birthday.

The colors of spring were what I found,
lavender and white blossoms nested
along stems,   and I lost my breath

to this abundance he, sitting half slack
in his chair, had wanted me
to have.   Why not
plentitude, he suggested

with flowers that filled my biggest vase,
and throbbed like memory does
on a summer afternoon
when through an open window
notes from an oboe
lift into the air.

My Father in the Mirror

A few hours before you died
you lumbered up in the hospital bed,
swung your good leg first to the floor,
facing the mirror,
and pointed to your razor.
Fearfully, as though asked for a sacrament,
I lathered where you pointed and drew
a smooth path along your patrician jaw.
Soon you would be ashes,
but now, you ran a finger under your chin,
and found a patch I had missed.

Summoned to account in the mirror
of every day, like you in the way the years
have set my less fine jaw,
today as the afternoon appears to settle
in the trees although it is moving,
          moving,

          I recall your finger
flagging the spot I had missed.
Holding my breath I helped you
get ready.

When the Words Come

I dream I have no power
in a hawk-hearted world.

Power of words I mean.
That mine are far from fire,

that the fire that could roar
is using twigs

and old tickets. That the letters
the pencil forms

in lines on the page
say nothing

you need to hear.
Look at these neat rows.

The baby has no words
yet his airy sighs

and soaring vowels
say everything I mean.

I copy him, I know
he's copying me, and I think,

oh woe when the words
come, they'll dive through you forever.

My Mother's Spoon

As I use it every day to stir honey into tea
your silver spoon acquires the amber
of tannin.

You were here
then not
that fast.

Stiff, lingering
between knowledge and belief,
my body goes on refusing this new world.
              Over and over

and over   it's true   then not
then true again
as all my bones recoil.

That moment
before
it's final
for real
I try to grip
as it gives way
to morning tea stirred and drunk with milk.

The Blessing

Today I spotted a Green Heron standing on one leg
while he unfurled one wing
at the river's edge.

Two days ago it was a Great Blue, tall and smoky,
still as a reed.   I would have called you
when I got home to say, hey,
two herons
in two days,

and now
I can't.   I'm left

with the breath-stopping vision of the elegant birds
in a new world.

Sorrow as Water

The way when it meets obstruction
        it pushes past   past stone   past
the dam laid across   past anything
   in the way of its pull
            to the space it took
                    such years to hollow.
Its nature
        is to fluctuate   to melt and freeze
rise
    and fall.

To think of sorrow as water is useful
    for the sorrowful.
                Though a pond in dank woods
        may grow fetid and clogged
it will neither last   nor die
        but be lifted
            by the breathing trees nearby
    which have need of its ingredients
            in their hunger to grow.

Measuring Cups

Now I stack my mother's measuring cups
by the kitchen sink.

There will always be the dent near the lip
of the small one,

and the careful line of wizened glue along a crack
in the vase she filled with peonies

when her youngest daughter married. How can I
part with what she used?

Her life in which a cup was dropped in argument
or haste, while blueberries

waited for sugar while the children played outside.
In which glue sufficed

for the umber vase from China. The tree forgets
a limb taken by wind,

wasps leave the leathery globe they labored to build.
I grant the given world its neutrality

but what of the remnants left in the things
that furnished her life?

In a village far from here, a gourd held water
poured over rice, a spoon

stirred as night filled a mud house.
Does some woman lift

the gourd that once held seeds then water
while she played,

does she pause in wonder that it remains
so shaped to hold the past?

You May Have Been

The quotidian tragedy
of motherhood is to hurt a child
unwittingly.

The tax levied by the life you tried
so hard to have was just the careful touch
I wouldn't do without.

You wanted to be
in some way acclaimed –

who doesn't
and as for the hurt
child who holds the self inside –
death comes

and here I am one morning
remembering my bike   how I flew
down Woodland Avenue
like a jet   no hands   so strong I knew my life
could matter

when over the handlebars I soared and smashed
on the street   and you may have come
with a warm washcloth
to clean the ground-up knees   blowing
while the Mercurochrome dried.

You may have
been that mother after all.
I forget.

Another Chance

though I make this up it is palpable
and not   as it once was   a beehive of loss

sensing you here so many years
after your death could feel hollow   a ghost

instead of this invisible sweater
I can wear in any season   ~
                                        just
today   as though you'd finally gotten through

to me   I see I am keeping you company
too   and more   as though your lingering

is not entirely my conjuring   but also that hungry
never avowed urge you had to hide

and be discovered
that made your armor necessary   ~   you thought

I was the one who could see   and thus we parried
and now it's all over but the chance

to know you better than you knew yourself
at last   ~   at last with nothing to lose

you want that   and I who feel you settling
inside me like a bird am comforted

you feel at home
and all it took to make it so was death

Consonants

     ga ga ga ga ga   says
the baby. "Trees," I say, "that's
a maple." I hand him a leaf,
he waves
     and crushes it. I follow up, "Look that one's
lost
  all
    its
     leaves," but he doesn't know
how to look where I point,   so he watches
me   make   sounds.

     ba ba ba ba ba ba   he says and I say
"Yes, you can pick
        up the gravel."
Since his small pink fingers can accomplish this,
he claps by waving both hands. I clap
too and lick the last of my latte foam.
"Let's go home," I say,
    turning the stroller.

    da da da da da
          Thank you,
           I think,
for a conversation that left
   nothing
     unsaid.

Reading to Finn

. . . on Thursday when Imogene woke up
she found she had grown antlers.
—David Small, ***Imogene's Antlers***

On every page she faces the obstacle
as though it isn't one,   caught on

the chandelier,   banging sideways through
the door,   the cook hangs doughnuts

on each branch and birds come,
everyone's curious except

her mother who faints and faints
and has to be carried to bed

and I think as I read,   Finn,
this is how the world

shows you motherhood –
let me tell you   but what would

I say,   let me tell you it tears
your heart out,   no   that's a secret

you try to keep while it grows
back   not innocent, not light,   but oh,

it grows back full

Another Morning Without God

The horizon
of the water was still
unbroken but sun had begun

to color up the clouds
in advance, and some high-riding
westerly cumulus

were luminous already
though not neighbors to the source
of light,

and I felt illumined too,
nearly desperate with gratitude
and no one to whom to bow.

I flung my arms
in an arc
acting out in lieu

of conversation charades
with God   this is Your love
the only teaching I heed.

Part III

These are the sparks

The Wick

In a field at an afternoon angle as sun
   yields to shadow   yearning rises
      like the moon   gaunt
               and delicious.

Goldenrod   sometimes
   waves when I pass.

I used to know You with childhood's
   fervor,   but then You never spoke however long
      I wandered
            in doubt.

   Or is Yours, finally, the language of the giant copper beech
that guards its leaves like coins
            in the gathering wind?

As though the distance I've always felt You keep
            is the wick,

and the immanence visible
            as blue heron poised across the river

or the way two silver clouds become one
         then two again,

as though
      these are the sparks.

Two by Two

Two snails,
two antelope,
two pigeons,

couple by couple
the wooden shell filled
by command, and borne up
on the lap of the flood.

And those coupled
with solitude,
what of them?

Didn't you call, Lord,
for the spirit to rise alone,
cleave to an untouchable
heavenly mate?
Didn't you offer your son
to walk alone
    on earth as our summons,
didn't he prepare for death alone
while others slept?

Among the secrets
You keep there is this one:
two by two looking out
to the sun
and the dove,
how they became
the saved?

"I look out the window"

the poet said
when asked how he starts to write.

I look out the window.   The same maple
is shaking its clinging leaves
        over
            the neighbor's house
                like ashes

                            yet nothing's
the same
    as yesterday.

Ocean Vuong Says of Robert Frost

He didn't see the ghosts

he *thought* these woods   he saw
stones dribbled in lines   left
by farms where sheep cropped until
the railroad opened the west
            and he wrote   he saw the old farms
old herders and mills   he put New England

into words we bought   and we saw
        we had a past insofar as   but being
who he was   descended from England
        and Scotland   he didn't see the ghosts
said the young Vietnamese poet
brought from Ho Chi Minh City as a child

        and he left the ghosts he didn't see
in the smoke of silence
        said the young poet   left them so he
could *think* the woods and we could
make them ours with sheep walls
        and sentinel trees

leaving their words in the air   Winnipesaukee
    Sunapee   Pennacook   Pautauckaway

tuck away is what he did with their fires drenched
    – families chased and shot –

whose woods these are I think I know
his house is in the village though

until we see them   the poet slight and quiet
in a chair says in his own words   they haunt

Sky Thick with Indecision

                    whether blue
       or sour metal will prevail   whether the snow
will cede to mud along the river filling fast ~

high vista,   be company
       to human turmoil   sway the trees into epithets worthy
of who we have become   move west as the nation

once did wild with greed
                              blow from the east
through the pores   of we who without cause
       expect fulfillment

"There's gonna be a doom"

is what the young Syrian who thought
he would get out says

to the journalist on the radio.
It's the kind of spring day

that rips you open
like a ripe fruit.

I park at the drugstore,
which ends the shelling

in the background of the broadcast,
and go through

the automatic door into
the cool interior for shampoo.

Burning Up

I lay in fever's lap
with rasping sighs, relieved to cancel life.

Stretched on the sofa I remembered how Violetta
lay melting as she hung on to say goodbye to Alfredo

and wondered what would I cling for ~
in a weakened state when *nothing*
is such a gripping word ~

eat nothing   do nothing   lie in that pyre
that's blazing through you and wonder what's worth
burning into nothing for ever again.

Walking Home on a Warm Evening

fists of cherry blossom jabbing
the night's spring wind

are a splash in the face   in a world
       unmoored   from its future
          while a curled child

  by an open window hears the whisper
of leaves as voices
  of assurance   and sinks
out of himself
  with ease and a whistling breath

At the Moment of Morning

    at the moment of morning when moon
  and cumulus are identically
 translucent,
for an instant
I behold
 what I take
  to be a cloud
   traced with some
    stellar compass   for an instant
      there is something   I call God

Two Messages for William Stafford

Every poem is a love poem
foraging for hope's marrow.

To marry silence,
ten thousand seeds

to the sky. A poem is hungry,
it roams alone   wanting

more than a friend,
a thread of its mute voice

to carry on through the trees
between mountains,

brushing leaves in a quiet way
that catches something

waiting to fall.
A kernel, a key.

Its work is never
done. You taught me that.

~ ~ ~ ~ ~ ~ ~

I turn to you
in bitter sadness.

Bent low
seeking ballast.

Something to grip as I move
foot by foot

through aisles of groceries.
Something to hold

to fill a chasm. I know
you know what I mean,

though you're gone
your breathing words

say only the heart of a mountain
is enough.

Lingering

         because clouds move
like music blown through shells

      and heaven is hung
on a comma of moon;

      because wind sweeps
the world grabbing seeds
   from the fields' stuporous grip,

      and feathers soft as smoke
settle with such fine fit
   around the thin bones of birds
they emerge in spring full of praise;

      because   as we strive
for dominion over all the world
   provides,

       look,
   the sun gradually
      flames every cloud
       in the sky

     and lingers

      before

        it leaves us

What if Faith

what if faith
came back
like a cat
after a few
rough nights
but in this case
decades?

Or is it among
the irretrievables,
like yesterday,
like my girlish knees,
or the passenger pigeon?

I Left It There

among splayed fountains of fern jetting up
along the river bank catching sun

as it escaped the mesh of oaks
and maples   among briars above the oval

oiled leaves of lilies barely bigger than grains
of rice   among jack in the pulpits

and vestiges of anemone   amid all this
new life I nearly stumbled

over a great decaying leg of wood   a birch
laid long ago on the forest floor

when it fell among its neighbors   I met it
right where it had forked

and though now mealy with remains
of the meals of all the insects

whose home it had been – borers caterpillars
and worms had moved to other tables

and left this body to its caverns – though
it smelled of all that dissipation

and dissolution I stood over   then bent
down   pulled back shags of bark

I looked under where tree and forest floor
were becoming one because I knew

there was something to see
about how little and how utterly we matter

and never have and always will and I left
it there as everything is left   meaning

it clung to me as I trudged out   and back up
the hill through the meadow

The Violet Hour,

when the eyes and back
turn upward from the desk, when the human engine waits . . .
—T. S. Eliot, "The Wasteland"

Among the lines hollow as bones
         three words . . .

internal frost of war-time   and how what's left
     decays   among the images
        of wasting lives he places
            the violet hour   the reader
        feels for a moment the hour

when the world is purple with fatigue
      another day   mist and shadow
blurring the hemlock's arms   the hour sighs
        over its own completion and in leaving
      transforms whatever's happened
            and hasn't . . .

briefly spreads a veil over every pointless
    or forgotten word or thought   briefly
        it calls the one
            by the window
or in the field back to the hearth lit at birth
                        tinder in hand

Late Summer

Pods of butterfly weed at the road edge
    split   spilling cargo
                              canoes
        of silk

Goldenrod: what was
    flame   now powder

Yielding every year
        to their departure

I open one hand –
    one closes.

A Lesson at Twilight

All day I pushed things around   pieces of paper   phrases
     dangling
         in my head   the dog underfoot

I zig-zagged in and out of the morose involuntary spell
  of a tired question   and then   in the late afternoon

I ran to the field across the street and into the aura
  of a golden maple

a torch at the verge of twilight   holding her quivering
  unconsummated own   against a blowing sky

Amends

I'm sorry
I say again
to the shards
of the blue plate

the soaked sill

the cat
by her empty bowl
too poised
to speak.

Forgiven by all
I turn
to the swaybacked
hemlock low with snow.

Maybe God Is This:

sand strewn with eel grass
and morning spume,

two oystercatchers strutting
ahead of my slow feet

until they squawk off
into the marsh and startle

a white egret who resumes
her stance still as stone

near a snail shell backside up
in marsh ooze,   its inside

the rose gold of some peach
still ripening in sun

somewhere else,   a shell here
and one there,

each a curved home
ready to crack and fall

into ivory pieces.

Bare Trees

I don't mind the geese
with their plangent one note leaving

for more sun, or the corn
getting big-toothed, the trees stripping

to the bone, their secrets intact
(how to break in wind and stand,

how to dress a wound
with ice).   I don't mean it's joyful

to be driven inward, to sit inside walls
watching ice slash down,

to move through the stillness of pots
and rugs lighting lamps,

to linger in pools of light
while the river groans locked in ice,

I mean it's real,
the way thought seeks a window

and passes irretrievably
through, the way it coats the bowl

of many salads, decades of greens
combined and eaten on decades

of plates all washed and stacked
like the towers of books with post cards

marking where they were discarded
or misplaced, it's real the way thought

relishes winter, its storms and wind
and nights deeply not of now.

Notes

"Neighbors": based on events recorded in the video documentary *Icyizere* by Patrick Mureithi, about a trauma healing group led by Rwandan Quakers.

"Encounter with a Mother in Rwanda": based on a meeting in Rwanda with the mother of a Congolese refugee in Florence, Massachusetts.

"Potatoes, Wood in Eastern Congo": witnessed in Goma, Eastern Democratic Republic of Congo.

"Some Writers in Burundi Compose a Radio Drama in Which the Past Is Present": description of a story writing workshop with the writers of Murikira Ukuri, a weekly radio drama broadcast in Burundi by Radio La Benevolencija.

"Sling the Statue": a familiar childhood game, evoked in the context of the national struggle over monuments to the past of this country.

"The Fence Inside": concerning the summer of 1961, during which the city of Lynchburg, Virginia closed its two segregated public pools in order to keep children of different races from being together, while simultaneously integrating the high schools.

"Ocean Vuong Says of Robert Frost": quoted lines from Frost's poem "Stopping by Woods on a Snowy Evening".

Acknowledgements

With appreciation to the editors of the following journals in which some of these poems were previously published:

2River View: "Maybe God is This" and "Measuring Cups"
Snowy Egret: "Another Morning Without God"
Silkworm 11: "Numbers"
Gallery of Writers Anthology: "But for her Clear Voice"
Thirty Poems in November 2017: "Consonants"
San Pedro River Review: "A Child in Virginia in the '50s"

With deep gratitude to Dorothy Barresi and Tebot Bach, for selecting this manuscript to receive the Patricia Bibby First Book Competition Prize. And especially to Beth Ruscio, who walked through these poems with me page by page, comma by comma, with unflagging patience, artistry, love of poetry, and attention to the smallest detail, helping me to realize it in a new and fuller way.

To the poets whose rich responses call to mind "It takes a village. . ." : Jean Blakeman, Libby Maxey, Sharon Tracey and Rebecca Olander, you're each in the architecture and spirit of these poems start to finish. Also Ellen Watson, Carol Edelstein, Robin Barber, Colleen Filler, Amy Gordon, Cynthia Snow, Beth Filson, Gail Thomas, and Holly Wren Spaulding, who have taught me so much through their feedback and their own work.

With gratitude to the family and friends who have been the home of my well-being as I write, whose responses to the poems in this book have helped me see them with new eyes. To my children Lucy and Nora, whose rich presence and true voices have shaped so much of who I am, and whose feedback I have sought and trusted always. And to their children, Finn and Gloria, who inspire poetry daily, and their husbands Nate and Akil. To my sisters, Pam, Laurie,

Nina and Meta, who've been my beloved friends and witnesses from birth, and among my sharpest readers. To my parents, Philip and Mary Elisabeth, who read poetry aloud to us from before we could speak. And always, to my friends, who accompany me in life, and have supported and encouraged me unfailingly in the mysterious process of putting words together. You're all in here somewhere.

About the Author

Adin Thayer has worked as a psychotherapist, a teacher at the Smith College School for Social Work, and a peacebuilding facilitator in several African countries. In addition to what she draws from these sources, her work queries her childhood growing up in Virginia when it was a legally segregated state. This background gives her work a sense of urgency as an adult to reveal, through her childhood eyes, a "not seeing" still inherent in the inequality we live with today. Threaded through her work is evidence of the multitude of resources, human, personal, cultural and spiritual, that people develop to transcend or transform challenging experiences. Among these resources, the lawfulness and beauty of the natural world have sustained and enriched her life, and are close to ubiquitous in her poetry. She was educated at Wellesley College and the University of North Carolina School for Social Work. She is the mother of two daughters and lives in Massachusetts.

TEBOT BACH
A 501 (c) (3) Literary Arts Education Non Profit

THE TEBOT BACH MISSION: advancing literacy, strengthening
community, and transforming life experiences with the power of poetry
through readings, workshops, and publications.

THE TEBOT BACH PROGRAMS
1. A poetry reading and writing workshop series for venues such as homeless
shelters, battered women's shelters, nursing homes, senior citizen daycare
centers, Veterans organizations, hospitals, AIDS hospices, correctional
facilities which serve under-represented populations. Participating poets
include: John Balaban, Brendan Constantine, Megan Doherty, Richard Jones,
Dorianne Laux, M.L. Leibler, Laurence Lieberman, Carol Moldaw, Patricia
Smith, Arthur Sze, Carine Topal, Cecilia Woloch.

2. A poetry reading and writing workshop series for the community Southern
California at large, and for schools K-University. The workshops feature
local, national, and international teaching poets; David St. John, Charles
Webb, Wanda Coleman, Amy Gerstler, Patricia Smith, Holly Prado, Dorothy
Lux, Rebecca Seiferle, Suzanne Lummis, Michael Datcher, B.H. Fairchild,
Cecilia Woloch, Chris Abani, Laurel Ann Bogen, Sam Hamill, David Lehman,
Christopher Buckley, Mark Doty.

3. A publishing component to give local, national, and international poets a
venue for publishing and distribution.

Tebot Bach
Box 7887
Huntington Beach, CA 92615-7887
714-968-0905
www.tebotbach.org